AMERICA
THE BEAUTIFUL

In the Words of
RALPH WALDO EMERSON

AMERICA THE BEAUTIFUL

by the Editors of COUNTRY BEAUTIFUL

Editorial Direction: Michael P. Dineen

Edited by Robert L. Polley

In the Words of

RALPH WALDO EMERSON

Published by Country Beautiful Corporation
Waukesha, Wisconsin

COUNTRY BEAUTIFUL: *Publisher and Editorial Director:* Michael P. Dineen; *Executive Editor:* Robert L. Polley; *Senior Editors:* Kenneth L. Schmitz, James H. Robb; *Associate Art Director:* Wilbur Howe; *Editorial Assistants:* Carolyn Muchhala, Lawrence Kenney, Janice M. Puta; *Executive Director, Sales and Marketing:* Richard W. Stone; *Production:* John Dineen; *Circulation Manager:* Trudy Schnittka; *Administrative Secretary:* Donna Griesemer; *Editorial Secretary:* Christine Maynard.

Country Beautiful Corporation is a wholly owned subsidiary of Flick-Reedy Corporation: *President:* Frank Flick; *Vice President and General Manager:* Michael P. Dineen; *Treasurer and Secretary:* Bok Robertson.

Frontispiece by Robert L. Olsen

CONTENTS

INTRODUCTION 8

I THE POET AND THE LAND 10

II THIS WIDEWORLD, AMERICA 26

III "LET THE MORNING BE" 46

IV A PRODIGALITY OF SEEDS 62

V A VISION OF THE WHOLE 70

VI "ALL THE TREES ARE WIND-HARPS" 82

INTRODUCTION

In today's tumultuous age, the bombastic style is in ascendance. Out of a desire to hold nothing back advocates on all sides have developed an inflated public rhetoric which obscures the truth more often than revealing it. In the writings of Ralph Waldo Emerson, the opposite is the case. In his essays and other formal writings, couched generally in abstract terms and an elevated style, are some of the most explosive ideas advanced by a distinguished American. At the same time, in his more spontaneous expressions, such as those in his Journal and elsewhere, he could speak quite frankly. For example, when he criticized Daniel Webster for his support of the Fugitive Slave Act: "The word *liberty* in the mouth of Mr. Webster sounds like the word *love* in the mouth of a courtesan. . . ."

Fundamentally, however, he was a man who lived and spoke gently, and his appearance and demeanor matched his language. This man with the slender, slightly stooped frame and thin, scholar's face with prominent nose was described by James Russell Lowell as having "a majesty about him beyond all other men I have ever known."

Born in 1803 to a family with many generations of service in the ministry, including Emerson's father, he entered Harvard College at the age of fourteen. Despite financial hardships brought on by his father's death when Emerson was eight, he graduated in four years. He taught school for a few years and then entered Harvard Divinity School. Upon completion of his formal education in 1829, he became a pastor in Boston and married a girl from New Hampshire who died only eighteen months later. Emerson, who had never had a great liking for formal religion, resigned his ministry in 1832 because of his views on a point of doctrine concerning the rite of the Lord's Supper.

Depressed by his wife's death and the death of a brother and in ill health himself, Emerson sailed for Europe. In Italy, where he admired the art treasures, his health returned, and he went to England where he met Coleridge, Wordsworth and Thomas Carlyle. On his return to America, he settled in the beautiful, old historic town of Concord, Massachusetts, and remarried. Here he spent the remaining forty-seven years of his life, growing in fame and wisdom under the combined influence of the town's charming setting, its historic past and an intellectual and social milieu that included Henry David Thoreau, Nathaniel Hawthorne and William Ellery Channing, and others.

Beginning in 1835, he spent six months each year lecturing. After polishing his lectures orally, he printed them as lectures. However, his first book,

Nature, published in 1836, was not a series of lectures, but genuine essays about the influence of nature on man, Emerson's nearest approach to a systematic approach to philosophy. The book was not enthusiastically received and his fame really began with two early addresses, "The American Scholar," before the Harvard Phi Beta Kappa Society in 1837, and the following year, his address to the graduating class of the Divinity School. In the first he said: "We have listened too long to the courtly muses of Europe." In the second he boldly appealed to the clergy to revise their theology and give their congregations original truths instead of traditional forms. Because of these views Emerson was denounced for his "revolutionary" thoughts and it was thirty years before Harvard invited him to speak there again.

Emerson's philosophy was given the label "transcendentalism," an unsatisfactory term whose vagueness displeased many in Emerson's time, including some who were called transcendentalists. Whatever the label, Emerson's ideas center around the "over-soul," the universal soul of which every living thing is a part. His transcendentalism, more poetry than formal philosophy, was based on a love of nature and a recognition that man is part of nature.

Thus Emerson was an American exponent of that movement in Western thought at the beginning of the nineteenth century known as romanticism, which held that a higher Reason beyond mere sense experience brought insight into ultimate truths. Through intuition the whole range of experience can be found in each man. By looking inward God can be found within the self. In Nature Emerson stated: "I become a transparent eyeball; I am nothing; I see all the currents of the Universal Being circulate through me. . . ."

But it is not for such ethereal flights into pure abstraction and generalizations about the ideal that Emerson is usually read today. It is for his shrewd observations and his penetrating perceptions of the solid world about him, as when he wrote: "I like dry light, and hard clouds, hard expressions, and hard manners," and "Society seems noxious. I believe that against these baleful influences Nature is the antidote. The man comes out of the wrangle of the shop and office, and sees the sky and woods, and is a man again. . . . But how few men see the sky and woods!"

One manifestation of his belief in the infinitude of the self was his faith in the potential of American democracy, still new to the world of Emerson's time. Of the 1830's and 1840's he said: "There was a new consciousness. The former generations acted under the belief that a shining social prosperity was the beautitude of man, and sacrificed uniformly to the State. The modern mind believed that the nation existed for the individual, for the guardianship and education of every man."

Emerson's dynamic beliefs and the eloquence with which he expressed them made him the great cultural liberator of his time, especially for young people. But unlike many heroes of the young who are soon forgotten, Emerson started reverberations that are still being felt today. Oliver Wendell Holmes called his "American Scholar" address "our intellectual Declaration of Independence," and his substantial influence over the younger Thoreau is well known. His call for an American poet of genius who "knew the value of our incomparable materials . . . as yet unsung," had a strong impact on Walt Whitman, one of our greatest poets, who sent Emerson a copy of his first book. And through Whitman his valuable legacy to American poetry continues to this day. The life of the mind in America and our entire cultural heritage turned a vital corner because of Ralph Waldo Emerson, the kindly and brilliant Sage of Concord.

— *Robert L. Polley*

The Poet and the Land

It was her [Nature's] stern necessity: all things
Are of one pattern made; bird, beast and flower,
Song, picture, form, space, thought, and character,
Deceive us, seeming to be many things,
And are but one.

XENOPHANES

By fate, not option, frugal Nature gave
One scent to hyson and to wallflower,
One sound to pine-groves and to waterfalls
One aspect to the desert and the lake.
It was her stern necessity: all things
Are of one pattern made; bird, beast and flower,
Song, picture, form, space, thought, and character,
Deceive us, seeming to be many things,
And are but one. Beheld far off, they part
As God and devil; bring them to the mind,
They dull its edge with their monotony.
To know one element, explore another,
And in the second reappears the first.
The specious panorama of a year
But multiplies the image of a day, —
A belt of mirrors round a taper's flame;
And universal Nature, through her vast
And crowded whole, an infinite paroquet,
Repeats one note.

From THE TITMOUSE

Miles off, three dangerous miles, is home;
Must borrow his winds who there would come.
Up and away for life! be fleet! —
The frost-king ties my fumbling feet,
Sings in my ears, my hands are stones,
Curdles the blood to the marble bones,
Tugs at the heart-strings, numbs the sense
And hems in life with narrowing fence.
Well, in this broad bed lie and sleep,
The punctual stars will vigil keep,
Embalmed by purifying cold,
The winds shall sing their dead-march old,
The snow is no ignoble shroud,
The moon thy mourner, and the cloud.

Softly, — but this way fate was pointing,
'Twas coming fast to such anointing,
When piped a tiny voice hard by,
Gay and polite, a cheerful cry,
Chic-chicadeedee! saucy note
Out of sound heart and merry throat,
As if it said, "Good day, good sir!
Fine afternoon, old passenger!
Happy to meet you in these places,
Where January brings few faces."

It was nature's stern necessity: all things are of one pattern made.

Robert Sena

12

*Thy summer voice, Musketaquit, repeats
the music of the rain . . .*

TWO RIVERS

Thy summer voice, Musketaquit,
Repeats the music of the rain;
But sweeter rivers pulsing fit
Through thee, as thou through Concord Plain.

Thou in thy narrow banks art pent:
The stream I love unbounded goes
Through flood and sea and firmament;
Through light, through life, it forward flows.

I see the inundation sweet,
I hear the spending of the stream
Through years, through men, through nature fleet,
Through love and thought, through power and dream.

Musketaquit, a goblin strong,
Of shard and flint makes jewels gay;
They lose their grief who hear his song,
And where he winds is the day of day.

So forth and brighter fares my stream,
Who drink it shall not thirst again;
No darkness stains its equal gleam,
And ages drop in it like rain.

*"I hear the spending of the stream
through years, through men, through nature fleet."*

"It seemed that Nature could not raise
A plant in any secret place, . . .
But he would come in the very hour
It opened in its virgin bower. . . ."

From WOODNOTES I

1

When the pine tosses its cones
To the song of its waterfall tones,
Who speeds to the woodland walks?
To birds and trees who talks?
Caesar of his leafy Rome
There the poet is at home.
He goes to the river-side, —
Not hook nor line hath he;
He stands in the meadows wide, —
Nor gun nor scythe to see.
Sure some god his eye enchants:
What he knows nobody wants.
In the wood he travels glad,
Without better fortune had,
Melancholy without bad. . . .

16

2

And such I knew, a forest seer,
A minstrel of the natural year,
Foreteller of the vernal ides,
Wise harbinger of spheres and tides,
A lover true, who knew by heart
Each joy the mountain dales impart;
It seemed that Nature could not raise
A plant in any secret place,
In quaking bog, on snowy hill,
Beneath the grass that shades the rill,
Under the snow, between the rocks,
In damp fields known to bird and fox.
But he would come in the very hour
It opened in its virgin bower,
As if a sunbeam showed the place,
And tell its long-descended race.

4

. . . 'You ask,' he said, 'what guide
Me through trackless thickets led,
Through thick-stemmed woodlands rough and wide.
I found the water's bed.
The watercourses were my guide;
I travelled grateful by their side,
Or through their channel dry;
They led me through the thicket damp,
Through brake and fern, the beavers' camp,
Through beds of granite cut my road,
And their resistless friendship showed.
The falling waters led me,
The foodful waters fed me,
And brought me to the lowest land,
Unerring to the ocean sand.
The moss upon the forest bark
Was pole-star when the night was dark;
The purple berries in the wood
Supplied me necessary food;
For Nature ever faithful is
To such as trust her faithfulness.
When the forest shall mislead me,
When the night and morning lie,
When sea and land refuse to feed me,
'T will be time enough to die;
Then will yet my mother yield
A pillow in her greenest field,
Nor the June flowers scorn to cover
The clay of their departed lover.'

"The falling waters led me,
The foodful waters fed me,
And brought me to the lowest land."

Helen Nestor

If eyes were made for seeing, then Beauty
is its own excuse for being . . .

From MAY-DAY

Daughter of Heaven and Earth, coy Spring,
With sudden passion languishing,
Maketh all things softly smile,
Painteth pictures mile on mile,
Holds a cup with cowslip wreaths,
Whence a smokeless incense breathes.

. . . .

What was that I heard
Out of the hazy land?
Harp of the wind, or song of bird,
Or clapping of shepherd's hands,
Or vagrant booming of the air,
Voice of a meteor lost in day?
Such tidings of the starry sphere
Can this elastic air convey.

THE RHODORA

In May, when sea-winds pierced our solitudes,
I found the fresh Rhodora in the woods,
Spreading its leafless blooms in a damp nook,
To please the desert and the sluggish brook.
The purple petals, fallen in the pool,
Made the black water with their beauty gay;
Here might the red-bird come his plumes to cool,
And court the flower that cheapens his array.
Rhodora! If the sages ask thee why
This charm is wasted on the earth and sky,
Tell them, dear, that if eyes were made for seeing,
Then Beauty is its own excuse for being:
Why thou wert there, O rival of the rose!
I never thought to ask, I never knew;
But, in my simple ignorance, suppose
The self-same Power that brought me there brought you.

T.D Lowes

"Daughter of Heaven and Earth, coy Spring, maketh all things softly smile."

Behold the Sea, the opaline, the plentiful and strong . . .

SEA-SHORE

I heard or seemed to hear the chiding Sea
Say, Pilgrim, why so late and slow to come?
Am I not always here, thy summer home?
Is not my voice thy music, morn and eve?
My breath thy healthful climate in the heats,
My touch thy antidote, my bay thy bath?
Was ever building like my terraces?
Was ever couch magnificent as mine?
Lie on the warm rock-ledges, and there learn
A little hut suffices like a town.
I make your sculptured architecture vain,
Vain beside mine. I drive my wedges home,
And carve the coastwise mountain into caves.
Lo! Here is Rome, and Nineveh, and Thebes,
Karnak, and Pyramid, and Giant's Stairs,
Half piled or prostrate; and my newest slab
Older than all they race.

                Behold the Sea,
The opaline, the plentiful and strong,
Yet beautiful as is the rose in June,
Fresh as the trickling rainbow of July;
Sea full of food, the nourisher of kinds,
Purger of earth, and medicine of men;
Creating a sweet climate by my breath,
Washing out harms and griefs from memory,
And, in my mathematic ebb and flow,
Giving a hint of that which changes not.
Rich are the sea-gods: — who gives gifts but they?
They grope the sea for pearls, but more than pearls:
They pluck Force thence, and give it to the wise.
For every wave is wealth to Daedalus,
Wealth to the cunning artist who can work
This matchless strength. Where shall he find, O waves!
A load your Atlas shoulders cannot lift?

I wish my hammer pounding evermore
The rocky coast, smite Andes into dust,
Strewing my bed, and, in another age,
Rebuild a continent of better men.
Than In unbar the doors: my paths lead out
The exodus of nations: I disperse
Men to all shores that front the hoary main.

Stoy for Alpha Photos

"I wish my hammer pounding evermore
The rocky coast, smite Andes into dust,
Strewing my bed, and, in another age,
Rebuild a continent of better men."

I too have arts and sorceries;
Illusion dwells forever with the wave.
I know what spells are laid. Leave me to deal
With credulous and imaginative man;
For, though he scoop my water in his palm,
A few rods off he deems it gems and clouds.
Planting strange fruits and sunshine on the shore,
I make some coast alluring, some lone isle,
To distant men, who must go there, or die.

21

This farm is mine, my children's and my name's . . .

HAMATREYA

Bulkeley, Hunt, Willard, Hosmer, Meriam, Flint,
Possessed the land which rendered to their toil
Hay, corn, roots, hemp, flax, apples, wool and wood.
Each of these landlords walked amidst his farm,
Saying, "Tis mine, my children's and my name's:
How sweet the west wind sounds in my own trees!
How graceful climb those shadows on my hill!
I fancy these pure waters and the flags
Know me, as does my dog: we sympathize;
And, I affirm, my actions smack of the soil."
Where are these men? Asleep beneath their grounds:
And strangers, fond as they, their furrows plough.
Earth laughs in flowers, to see her boastful boys
Earth-proud, proud of the earth which is not theirs;
Who steer the plough, but cannot steer their feet
Clear of the grave.
They added ridge to valley, brook to pond,
And sighed for all that bounded their domain;
"This suits me for a pasture; that's my park;
We must have clay, lime, gravel, granite-ledge,
And misty lowland, where to go for peat.
The land is well — lies fairly to the south.
Tis good, when you have crossed the sea and back,
To find the sitfast acres where you left them."
Ah! the hot owner sees not Death, who adds
Him to his land, a lump of mold the more.
Hear what the Earth says: —

Earth-Song

"Mine and yours;
Mine, not yours.
Earth endures;
Stars abide —
Shine down in the old sea;
Old are the shores;
But where are old men?
I who have seen much,
Such have I never seen.

"The lawyer's deed
Ran sure,
In tail,
To them, and to their heirs
Who shall succeed,
Without fail,
Forevermore.

"Here is the land, shaggy with wood,
With its old valley, Mound and flood."

T.D. Lowes

"Earth laughs in flowers, to see her boastful boys earth-proud, proud of the earth which is not theirs"

"Here is the land,
Shaggy with wood,
With its old valley,
Mound and flood.
But the heritors?
Fled like the flood's foam, —
The lawyer, and the laws,
And the kingdom,
Clean swept herefrom.

"They called me theirs,
Who so controlled me;
Yet every one
Wished to stay, and is gone,
How am I theirs,
If they cannot hold me,
But I hold them?"
When I heard the Earth-song
I was no longer brave;
My avarice cooled
Like lust in the chill of the grave.

Robert Se

"Think me not unkind and rude
That I walk alone in grove and glen;
I go to the god of the wood
To fetch his word to men."

From EACH AND ALL

Nothing is fair or good alone.
I thought the sparrow's note from heaven,
Singing at dawn on the alder bough;
I brought him home, in his nest, at even:
He sings the song, but it cheers not now.
For I did not bring home the river and sky;
He sang to my ear — they sang to my eye.
The delicate shells lay on the shore;
The bubbles of the latest wave
Fresh pearls to their enamel gave,
And the bellowing of the savage sea
Greeted their safe escape to me.

24

I wiped away the weeds and foam,
I fetched my sea-born treasures home;
But the poor, unsightly, noisome things
Had left their beauty on the shore
With the sun and the sand and the wild uproar.
. . . .
Then I said, "I covet truth;
Beauty is unripe childhood's cheat;
I leave it behind with the games of youth." —
As I spoke, beneath my feet
The ground-pine curled its pretty wreath,
Running over the club-moss burrs;
I inhaled the violet's breath;
Around me stood the oaks and firs;
Pine cones and acorns lay on the ground;
Over me soared the eternal sky,
Full of light and of deity;
Again I saw, again I heard,
The rolling river, the morning bird; —
Beauty through my senses stole;
I yielded myself to the perfect whole.

THE APOLOGY

Think me not unkind and rude
    That I walk alone in grove and glen;
I go to the god of the wood
    To fetch his word to men.

Tax not my sloth that I
    Fold my arms beside the brook;
Each cloud that floated in the sky
    Writes a letter in my book.

Chide me not, laborious band,
    For the idle flowers I brought;
Every aster in my hand
    Goes home loaded with a thought.

There was never mystery
    But 'tis figured in the flowers;
Was never secret history
    But birds tell it in the bowers.

One harvest from thy field
    Homeward brought the oxen strong;
A second crop thine acres yield,
    Which I gather in a song.

II
This Wideworld, America

We will walk on our own feet; we will work with our own hands; we will speak our own minds. . . .A nation of men will for the first time exist because each believes himself inspired by the Divine Soul which also inspires all men.

"At midday, the vertical sun was perpendicular to the cavity, and poured its full effulgence upon the mirror floor."

In aforetime, while to the inhabitants of Europe, the existence of America was yet a secret in the heart of time, there dwelled a Giant upon the South Mountain Chimborazo, who extended a beneficient dominion over hills and clouds and continents, and sustained a communication with his mother — Nature. He lived two hundred years in that rich land, causing peace and justice, and he battled with the Mammoths, and slew them. Upon the summit of the mountain, amid the snows of all the winters, was the mouth of a cave which was lined with golden ore. This cavity,

28

Nature fashioned the mighty tenement, for the bower of her son. . .

termed "The Golden Lips," admitted downwards into the centre of the mountain which was a vast and spacious temple, and all its walls and ceilings glowing with pure gold. Man had never polluted it with his tools of art. Nature fashioned the mighty tenement, for the bower of her son. At midday, the vertical sun was perpendicular to the cavity, and poured its full effulgence upon the mirror floor; its reflected beams blazed on all sides from the fretted roof, with a lustre which eclipsed the elder glory of the temple of Solomon. In the centre of this gorgeous palace, bareheaded and alone, the Giant Californ performed the incommunicable rite, and studied the lines of destiny. When the sun arrived at the meridian, a line of light traced this inscription upon the wall — "A thousand years, A thousand years, and the Hand shall come, and shall tear the Veil for all." Two thousand years have passed, the mighty progress of improvement & civilization have been forming the force which shall reveal Nature to Man. To roll about the outskirts of this Mystery and ascertain and describe its pleasing wonders — be this the journey of my Wideworld. The Hand shall come; — I traced its outline in the mists of the morning.

Journal, 1822

Is it not the chief disgrace in the world, not to be an unit — not to be reckoned one character — not to yield that peculiar fruit which each man was created to bear, but to be reckoned in the gross, in the hundred, or the thousand, of the party, the section, to which we belong; and our opinion predicted geographically, as the north, or the south? Not so, brothers and friends — please God, ours shall not be so. We will walk on our own feet; we will work with our own hands; we will speak our own minds. The study of letters shall be no longer a name for pits, for doubt, and for sensual indulgence. The dread of man and the love of man shall be a wall of defence and a wreath of joy around all. A nation of men will for the first time exist, because each believes himself inspired by the Divine Soul which also inspires all men.

From "The American Scholar," Lecture, 1837

S.J. Krasemann

A Jack-in-the-pulpit unsheathes with early spring energy in a green woodland.

Let us live in America, too thankful for our want of feudal institutions. Our houses and towns are like mosses and lichens, so slight and new; but youth is a fault of which we shall daily mend. [This land] too is as old as the Flood, and wants no ornament or privilege which nature could bestow. Here stars, here woods, here hills, here animals, here men abound, and the vast tendencies concur of a new order. If only the men are employed in conspiring with the designs of the Spirit who led us hither and is leading us still, we shall quickly enough advance out of all hearing of others' censures, out of all regrets of our own, into a new and more excellent social state than history has recorded.

From "The Young American," Lecture, 1884

This land wants no ornament or privilege which nature could bestow. . .

The settler ceases to be an ordinary adventurer, providing for himself, but becomes the representative of human nature.

It was to be expected that America should bring to the conflict unwonted national energy from the invigorating solitudes of her clime. We look with confident expectation for something extraordinary by word or deed in the primitive settlers of a large and fruitful territory. For there is a charm in nature that constrains her to render up a sevenfold blessing of health and life to him who inhales the first breath of her virgin air, and an abundant harvest to him who hath first laid the chain of cultivation upon the unbroken strength and freedom of the soil. There is certainly something deeply interesting in the history of one who invades the coast of an unknown continent and first breaks the silence which hath reigned there since the creation. As he goes alone to the wilderness and sets his axe to the root of the forest and we reflect that this stroke which echoes through the wood begins a dominion which shall never end till this green and silent woodland shall groan beneath the feet of countless multitudes and shall exchange the frequent solitary warble of a bird for the noise of nations, the outcry of human passion, and the groan of human misery. Under these views the settler ceases to be an ordinary adventurer, providing for himself and his son, or his friends, — but becomes the representative of human nature, the father of the country, and, in a great measure, the arbiter of its future destinies, for many generations. We listen to hear the voice of nature in the sighing of the breeze; we listen for the complaint of Faun, and Dryad, — ''Art thou come hither also?'' But we moreover look for some signal manifestation of greatness in the subsequent story of the adventurer. His condition is so inspiring to the human faculties, that we anticipate a rapid and perfect development of them which shall outstrip the ordinary progress of man and send forward over the forest the spirit of civilization and science with unrivalled energy.

Journal, 1822

The American artist who would carve a wood-god, and who was familiar with the forest in Maine, where enormous fallen pine trees "cumber the forest floor," where huge mosses depending from the trees and the mass of the timber give a savage and haggard strength to the grove, would produce a very different statue from the sculptor who only knew a European woodland — the tasteful Greek, for example.

Journal, September 13, 1837

The solitary farmhouse displays to you the same mingled picture of frankness and meanness which are encompassed with brick walls in the city.

George T. Manna

If a man could go into the country but once, as to some raree shew, or if it were indulged by God but to a single individual to behold the majesty of nature, I think the credit and magnificence of art would fall suddenly to the ground. For take away the cheapness and ease of acquisition which lessen our estimation of its value, and who could suddenly find himself, alone in the green fields where the whole firmament meets the eye at once, and the pomp of woods and clouds and hills is poured upon the mind — without an unearthly animation? Upon a mountain-solitude a man instantly feels a sensible exaltation and a better claim to his rights in the universe. He who wanders in the woods perceives how natural it was to pagan imagination to find gods in every deep grove and by each fountain head. Nature seems to him not to be silent but to be eager and striving to break out into music. Each tree, flower, and stone, he invests with life and character; and it is impossible that the wind which breathes so expressive a sound amid the leaves — should mean nothing. But so striking is the ordination of Providence with regard to the uniformity of human character, that its traits seem to be hardly affected by such wide difference in circumstances as a town and country education. The change from one situation to the other may produce great alterations but the difference of life, little. The embowered cottage and solitary farmhouse display to you the same mingled picture of frankness and meanness, pride and poverty of feeling, fraud and charity, which are encompassed with brick walls in the city. Every pleasant feature is balanced by somewhat painful. To the stranger, the simplicity of manners is delightful and carries the memory back to the Arcadian reign of Saturn; and the primitive custom of saluting every passenger, is an agreeable acknowledgement of common sympathies, and a common nature. But from the want of an upper class in society, from the admirable republican equality which levels one with all, results a rudeness and sometimes a savageness of manners which is apt to disgust a polished and courtly man.

Journal, June 9, 1822

Philip Steinmetz

On the way to Winchester, whither our host accompanied us in the afternoon, my friends asked many questions respecting American landscapes, forest, houses — my house, for example. It is not easy to answer these queries well. There, I thought, in America, lies nature sleeping, overgrowing, almost conscious, too much by half for man in the picture, and so giving a certain *tristesse,* like the rank vegetation of swamps and forest seen at night, steeped in dews and rains, which it loves; and on it man seems not able to make much impression. There, in that great sloven continent, in high Allegheny pastures, in the sea-wide sky-skirted prairie, still sleeps and murmurs and hides the great mother, long since driven away from the trim hedge-rows and over-cultivated garden of England. And, in England, I am quite too sensible of this. Everyone is on his good behavior and must be dressed for dinner at six. So I put off my friends with very inadequate details, as best I could.

From ENGLISH TRAITS

33

Villager, FPG

The deep echoing aboriginal woods are not indifferent to any passenger.

The noonday darkness of the American forest, the deep, echoing, aboriginal woods, where the living columns of the oak and fir tower up from the ruins of the trees of the last millennium; where, from year to year, the eagle and the crow see no intruder; the pines, bearded with savage moss, yet touched with grace by the violets at their feet; the broad, cold lowland which forms its coat of vapor with the stillness of subterranean crystallization; and where the traveller, amid the repulsive plants that are native in the swamp, thinks with pleasing terror of the distant town; this beauty, haggard and desert beauty, which the sun and the moon, the snow and the rain, repaint and vary, has never been recorded by art, yet is not indifferent to any passenger.

From "Literary Ethics," Lecture, 1838

The noonday darkness of the
American forest has never been recorded by art. . .

Nation of Nantucket makes its own war and peace. Place of winds, bleak, shelterless, and, when it blows, a large part of the island is suspended in the air and comes into your face and eyes as if it was glad to see you. The moon comes here as if it was at home, but there is no shade.

Journal, May 23, 1847

. . . At last, we . . . entered the Mississippi. It is one of the great river landscapes of the world, wide wide eddying waters, low shores. The great river takes in the Ohio which had grown so large, turns it all to its own mud color, and does not become perceptibly larger.

The great sweeps of the Mississippi, the number of its large islands made and unmade in short periods, your distance from either shore, and the unvarying character of the green wilderness on either side from hour to hour, from day to day — the loneliest river — no towns, no houses, no dents in the forest, no boats almost — we met I believe but one steamboat in the first hundred miles — now and again then we notice a flat wood boat lying under the shore, blow our whistle, ring our bell, and near the land, then out of some log-shed appear black or white men, and hastily put out their boat, a large mud-scow, loaded with corded wood. . . . Then there were planters traveling, one with his family of slaves (6 blacks); peaceable looking farmer-like men who when they stretch themselves in the pauses of conversation disclose the butts of their pistols in their breast-pockets.

Letter to Lidian Emerson

Place of winds, bleak, shelterless.
The moon comes as if it was at home,
but there is no shade.

S.J. Kragemann

America is incomplete. Room for us all, since it has not ended, in bard or hero . . .

"The beautiful is never plentiful. On the whole, I say to myself that our conditions in America are not easier or less expensive than the European."

America is incomplete. Room for us all, since it has not ended, nor given sign of ending, in bard or hero. 'Tis a wild democracy, the riot of mediocrities, and none of your selfish Italies and Englands, where an age sublimates into a genius, and the whole population is made into Paddies to feed his porcelain veins, by transfusion from their brick arteries. Our few fine persons are apt to die. . . . Nature has only so much force, and must dilute it, if it is to be multiplied into millions. "The beautiful is never plentiful." On the whole, I say to myself, that our conditions in America are not easier or less expensive than the European.

Letter to Thomas Carlyle

John M. Zielins

36

George T. Manna

For walking, you must have a broken country. In Illinois, everybody rides. There is no good walk in that state. The reason is, a square yard of it is as good as a hundred miles. You can distinguish from the cows a horse feeding, at the distance of five miles, with a naked eye. Hence, you have the monotony of Holland, and when you step out of the door can see all that you will have seen when you come home. In Massachusetts, our land is agreeably broken, and is permeable like a park, and not like some towns in the more broken country of New Hampshire, built on three or four hills having each one side at forty-five degrees and the other side perpendicular: so that if you go a mile, you have only the choice whether you will climb the hill on your way out or on your way back. The more reasons we have to be content with the felicity of our slopes in Massachusetts, undulating, rocky, broken and surprising, but without this alpine inconveniency. Twenty years ago in northern Wisconsin the pinery was composed of trees so big, and so many of them, that it was impossible to walk in the country, and the traveler had nothing for it but to wade in the streams. One more inconveniency, I remember, they showed me in Illinois, that, in the bottom lands, the grass was fourteen feet high.

From COUNTRY LIFE

37

I have been something of a traveller the last year...

There is very little in this village to be said to you, and, with all my love of your letters, I think it the kind part to defend you from our imbecilities, — my own, and other men's. Besides, my eyes are bad, and prone to mutiny at any hint of white paper.

And yet I owe you all my story, of story I have. I have been something of a traveller the last year, and went down the Ohio River to its mouth; walked nine miles into, and nine miles out of the Mammoth Cave, in Kentucky, — walked or sailed, — for we cross small underground streams, — and lost one day's light: then steamed up the Mississippi, five days, to Galena. In the upper Mississippi, you are always in a lake with many islands. "The Far West" is the right name for these verdant deserts. On all the shores, interminable silent forest. If you land, there is prairie behind prairie, forest behind forest, sites of nations, no nations. The raw bullion of nature, what we call "moral" value not yet stamped on it. But in a thousand miles the immense material values will show twenty or fifty Californias; that a good ciphering head will make one where he is. Thus at Pittsburgh, on the Ohio, the Iron City, whither, from want of railroads, few Yankees have penetrated, every acre of land has three or four bottoms, first of rich soil; then nine feet of bituminous coal; a little lower, fourteen feet of coal; then iron, or salt; salt springs with a valuable oil called petroleum, floating on their surface. Yet this acre sells for the price of any tillage acre in Massachusetts; and, in a year, the railroads will reach it, east and west. — I came home by the great northern lakes & Niagara.

Letter to Thomas Carlyle, 1851

Good rides to you and the longest escapes from London streets! I too have a new plaything, the best I ever had — a woodlot. Last fall I bought a piece of more than forty acres on the border of a little lake half a mile wide and more, called Walden Pond — a place to which my feet have for years been accustomed to bring me once or twice in a week at all seasons. My lot to be sure is on the further side of the water, not so familiar to me as the nearer shore. Some of the wood is an old growth, but most of it has been cut off within twenty years and is growing thriftily. In these May days, when maples poplars oaks birches walnut and pine are in

The Red River, Menisee County, Kentucky.

their spring glory, I go thither every afternoon, and cut with my hatchet an Indian path through the thicket all along the bold shore, and open the finest pictures. My two little girls know the road now though it is nearly two miles from my house and find their way to the spring at the foot of a pine grove and with some awe to the ruins of a village of shanties all overgrown with mullein which the Irish who built the railroad left behind them. At a good distance in from the shore the land rises to a rocky head, perhaps sixty feet above the water. Thereon I think to place a hut, perhaps it will have two stories and be a petty tower, looking out to Monadnoc and other New Hampshire Mountains. There I hope to go with book and pen when good hours come. I shall think there, a fortnight might bring you from London to Walden Pond. — Life wears on, and do you say the grey hairs appear? Few can so well afford them.

Letter to Thomas Carlyle, 1846

In one of his letters to Thomas Carlyle, Emerson described the geography of the West, its high mountains which reach "the altitude of Mont Blanc."

California surprises with a geography, climate, vegetation, beasts, birds, fishes even, unlike ours; the land immense; the Pacific Sea; steam brings the near neighborhood of Asia; and South America at your feet; the mountains reaching the altitude of Mont Blanc; the state in its 600 miles of latitude producing all our Northern fruits, and also the fig, orange, and banana. But the climate chiefly surprised me. The almanac said April; but the day said June; — day after day for six weeks uninterrupted sunshine. November and December are the rainy months. The whole country was colored with flowers, and all of them unknown to us except in greenhouses. Every bird that I know at home is represented here, but in gayer plumes. On the plains we saw multitudes of antelopes, hares, gophers — even elks, and one pair of

40

wolves on the plains; the grizzly bear only in a cage. We crossed one region of the buffalo, but only saw one captive. We found Indians at every railroad station, — the squaws and papooses begging, and the "bucks" as they wickedly call them, lounging. On our way out, we left the Pacific RR. for 24 hours to visit Salt Lake: called on Brigham Young — just 70 years old — who received us with quiet uncommitting courtesy, at first, — a strong-built, self-possessed, sufficient man with plain manners. He took early occasion to remark that "the one-man-power really meant all-men's-power." Our interview was peaceable enough, and rather mended my impression of the man. . . .

Letter to Thomas Carlyle, 1871

I go twice a week over to Concord with Ellery, and, as we sit on the steep park at Conantum, we still have the same regret as oft before. Is all this beauty to perish? Shall none remake this sun and wind, the sky-blue river, the river-blue sky, the yellow meadow spotted with sacks and sheets of cranberry-pickers; the red bushes; the iron-gray house with just the color of the granite rock; the paths of the thicket, in which the only engineers are the cattle grazing on yonder hill? . . . Whole zones and climates she has concentrated into apples. We think of the old benefactors who have conquered these fields. . . .

Journal, September 1848

"Shall none remake this sun and wind, the sky-blue river, the river-blue sky, the yellow meadow. . . ."

Helen Nestor

The horizon line marched by hills tossing like waves in a storm . . .

Climate has much to do with it — climate and race. Set a New Englander to describe any accident which happened in his presence. What hesitation and reserve in his narrative! He tells with difficulty some particulars, and gets as fast as he can to the result, and though he cannot describe, hopes to suggest the whole scene. Now listen to a poor Irishwoman recounting some experience of hers. Her speech flows like a river — so unconsidered, so humorous, so pathetic, such justice done to all parts! It is a true transubstantiation — the fact converted into speech, all warm and colored and alive, as it fell out. Our Southern people are almost all speakers, and have every advantage over the New England people, whose climate is so cold that 'tis said we do not like to open our mouths very wide.

From SOCIETY AND SOLITUDE

'Tis the coldest November I have ever known. This morning the mercury is at 26. Yesterday afternoon cold, fine ride with Ellery to Sudbury Inn, and mounted the side of Nobscot. Finest picture through wintry air of the russet Massachusetts. The landscape is democratic, not gathered into one city or baronial castle, but equally scattered into these white steeples, round which a town clusters in every place where six roads meet, or where a river branches or falls, or where the pan of soil is a little deeper. The horizon line marched by hills tossing like waves in a storm; firm indigo line. 'Tis a pretty revolution which is effected in the landscape by simply turning your head upside down, or, looking through your legs: in infinite softness and loveliness is added to the picture. It changes the landscape at once from November to June, or, as Ellery declared, makes *Campagna* of it at once; so, he said, *Massachusetts is Italy upside down.*

Journal, November 14, 1848

We have the finest climate in the world . . . in Massachusetts. If we have coarse days, and dog days, and white days, and days that are like ice-blinks, we have also yellow days, and crystal days — days which are neither hot nor cold, but the perfection of temperature. New England has a good climate — yet, in choosing a farm, we like a southern exposure, whilst Massachusetts, it must be owned, is on the northern slope towards the Arctic circle and the Pole. Our climate is a series of surprises, and among our many prognostics of the weather, the only trustworthy one that I know is that, when it is warm, it is a sign that it is going to be cold.

From COUNTRY LIFE

S.J. Krasemann

" 'Tis the coldest November I have ever known. This morning the mercury is at 26."

. . . The apple is our national fruit. In October, the country is covered with its ornamental harvests. The American sun paints itself in these glowing balls amid the green leaves, the social fruit, in which Nature has deposited every possible flavor; whole zones and climates she has concentrated into apples. I am afraid you do not understand values. Look over the fence at the farmer who stands there. He makes every cloud in the sky, and every beam of the sun, serve him. His trees are full of brandy. He saves every drop of sap, as if it were wine. A few years ago those trees were whipsticks. Now, every one of them is worth a hundred dollars. Observe their form; not a branch nor a twig is to spare. They look as if they were arms and fingers, holding out to you balls of fire and gold. One tree yields the rent of an acre of land. Yonder pear has every property which should belong to a tree. It is hardy, and almost immortal. It accepts every species of nourishment, and yet could live, like an Arab, on air and water.

From COUNTRY LIFE

43

This time, like all times, is a good one,
if we but know what to do with it . . .

In New York lately, as in cities generally, one seems to lose all substance, and become surface in a world of surfaces. Everything is external, and I remember my hat and coat, and all my other surfaces, and nothing else. If suddenly a reasonable question is addressed to me, what refreshment and relief! I visited twice and parted with a most polite lady without giving her reason to believe that she had met any other in me than a worshipper of surfaces, like all Broadway. It stings me yet.

Journal, March 20, 1842

I hear the whistle of the locomotive in the woods. Wherever that music comes it has its sequel. It is the voice of the civility of the nineteenth century saying, "Here I am." It is interrogative: it is prophetic: and this Cassandra is believed: "Whew! Whew! Whew! How is real estate here in the swamp and wilderness? Ho for Boston! Whew! Whew! Down with that forest on the side of the hill. I want ten thousand chestnut sleepers. I want cedar posts, and hundreds of thousands of feet of boards. Up! My master of oak and pine! You have waited long enough — a good part of a century in the wind and stupid sky. Ho for axes and saws, and away with me to Boston! Whew! Whew! I will plant a dozen houses on this pasture next moon, and a village anon; and I will sprinkle yonder square mile with white houses like the broken snowbanks that strow it in March."

Journal, December 1842

Our age is bewailed as the age of introversion. Must that needs be evil? We, it seems, are critical; we are embarrassed with second thoughts; we cannot enjoy any thing for hankering to know whereof the pleasure consists; we are lined with eyes; we see with our feet; the time is infected with Hamlet's unhappiness, —
"Sicklied o'er with the pale cast of thought."
Is it so bad then? Sight is the last thing to be pitied. Would we be blind? Do we fear lest we should outsee nature and God, and drink truth dry? I look upon the discontent of the literary class as a mere announcement of the fact that they

Rohn Engh

" If there is any period one would desire to be born in, is it not the age of Revolution; when the old and the new stand side by side . . . "

find themselves not in the state of mind of their fathers, and regret the coming state as untried; as a boy dreads the water before he has learned that he can swim. If there is any period one would desire to be born in, is it not the age of Revolution; when the old and the new stand side by side and admit of being compared; when the energies of all men are searched by fear and by hope; when the historic glories of the old can be compensated by the rich possibilities of the new era? This time, like all times, is a very good one, if we but know what to do with it.

From "The American Scholar," Lecture, 1837

45

III
"Let the Morning Be"

We are as much strangers in nature as we are aliens from God. We do not understand the notes of birds. . . .

You must treat the days respectfully, you must be a day yourself . . .

To speak truly, few adult persons can see nature. Most persons do not see the sun. At least they have a very superficial seeing. The sun illuminates only the eye of the man, but shines into the eye and the heart of the child. The lover of nature is he whose inward and outward senses are still truly adjusted to each other; who has retained the spirit of infancy even into the era of manhood. His intercourse with heaven and earth becomes part of his daily food. In the presence of nature a wild delight runs through the man, in spite of real sorrows. Nature says — he is my creature, and maugre all his impertinent griefs, he shall be glad with me.

From NATURE

. . . You must treat the days respectfully, you must be a day yourself, and not interrogate it like a college professor. The world is enigmatical — everything said, and everything known or done — and must not be taken literally, but genially. We must be at the top of our condition to understand anything rightly. You must hear the bird's song without attempting to render it into nouns and verbs. Cannot we be a little abstemious and obedient? Cannot we let the morning be?

From SOCIETY AND SOLITUDE

"The sun illuminates only the eye of the man, but shines into the eye and the heart of the child."

Rohn Engh

Every day shows a new thing to veteran walkers. Yesterday reflections of trees in the ice: snowflakes, perfect rowels, on the ice; beautiful groups of icicles all along the eastern shore of Flint's Pond, in which, especially where encrusting the bough of a tree, you have the union of the most flowing with the most fixed.

Journal, December 14, 1849

A thaw for more than a week and three days of heavenly weather, bringing all mythology on their breezy dawns. Down falls the water from the steeps; up shoots the northern light after sunset from the horizon. But Nature seems a dissipated hussy. She seduces us from all work; listen to her rustling leaves — to the invitations which each blue peak and rolling river and fork of woodland road offers — and we should never wield the shovel or the trowel.

Journal, February 26, 1845

Opposite: *"Down falls the water from the steeps; . . ."*

We do not know the uses
of more than a few plants . . .

A susceptible person does not like to indulge his tastes in this kind, without the apology of some trivial necessity; he goes to see a wood-lot, or to look at the crops, or to fetch a plant or a mineral from a remote locality, or he carries a fowling-piece, or a fishing-rod. I suppose this shame must have a good reason. A dilettantism in nature is barren and unworthy. The fop of fields is no better than his brother of Broadway.

From "Nature," ESSAYS: SECOND SERIES

There is no more brilliant autumn red than the berries of the Jack-in-the-pulpit.

S.J. Krasemann

The world proceeds from the same spirit as the body of man. It is a remoter and inferior incarnation of God, a projection of God in the unconscious. But it differs from the body in one important respect. It is not, like that, now subjected to the human will. Its serene order is inviolable by us. It is, therefore, to us, the present expositor of the divine mind. It is a fixed point whereby we may measure our departure. As we degenerate, the contrast between us and our house is more evident. We are as much strangers in nature as we are aliens from God. We do not understand the notes of birds. The fox and the deer run away from us; the bear and tiger rend us. We do not know the uses of more than a few plants, as corn and the apple, the potato and the vine. Is not the landscape, every glimpse of which hath a grandeur, a face of him? Yet this may show us what discord is between man and nature, for you cannot freely admire a noble landscape if laborers are digging in the field hard by. The poet finds something ridiculous in his delight until he is out of the sight of men.

From NATURE

A man must saunter and sleep and be inferior and silly.

Journal, June 8, 1838

Pope and Johnson and Addison write as if they had never seen the face of the country, but had only read of trees and rivers in books.

Pope and Johnson and Addison write as if they had never seen the face of the country, but had only read of trees and rivers in books. The striped fly that eats our squash and melon vines, the rosebug, the corn worm, the red old leaf of the vines that entices the eye to new search for the lurking strawberry, the thicket and little bowers of the pea-vine, the signs of ripeness and all the hints of the garden, these grave city writers never knew. The towers of white blossoms which the chestnut tree uplifts in the landscape in July, the angle of strength (almost a right angle), at which the oak puts out its iron arms; the botany of the meadows and water sides — what had Queen Anne's wits to do with these creatures? Did they ever prick their fingers with a thorn of a gooseberry? Did they ever hear the squeak of a bat or see his flitting?

Journal, July 29, 1837

Robert Sena

"But a loud singer, or a storyteller, or a vain talker profanes the river and the forest, and is nothing like so good company as a dog."

Few men know how to take a walk. The qualifications of a professor are endurance, plain clothes, old shoes, an eye for nature, good humor, vast curiosity, good speech, good silence and nothing too much. If man tells me that he has an intense love of nature, I know, of course, that he has none. Good observers have the manners of trees and animals, their patient good sense, and if they add words, 'tis only when words are better than silence. But a loud singer, or a storyteller, or a vain talker profanes the river and the forest, and is nothing like so good company as a dog.

From COUNTRY LIFE

We know more from nature
than we can at will communicate. . .

The mystery of nature was never displayed more happily. The corn and the wine have been freely dealt to all creatures, and the never-broken silence with which the old bounty goes forward has not yielded yet one word of explanation. One is constrained to respect the perfection of this world in which our senses converse. How wide; how rich; what invitation from every property it gives to every faculty of man! In its fruitful soils; in its navigable sea in its mountains of metal and stone; in its forest of all woods; in its animals; in its chemical ingredients; in the powers and path of light, heat, attraction and life, it is well worth the pith and heart of great men to subdue and enjoy it.

From An address delivered before the Senior Class at Divinity College, Cambridge, July 1838

Only as far as the masters of the world have called in nature to their aid, can they reach the height of magnificence.

From "Nature," ESSAYS: SECOND SERIES

These facts may suggest the advantage which the country-life possesses, for a powerful mind, over the artificial and curtailed life of cities. We know more from nature than we can at will communicate. Its light flows into the mind evermore, and we forget its presence. The poet, the orator, bred in the woods, whose senses have been nourished by their fair and appeasing changes year after year, without design and without heed — shall not lose their lesson altogether, in the roar of cities or the broil of politics. Long hereafter, amidst agitation and terror in national councils — in the hour of revolution — these solemn images shall reappear in their morning lustre, as fit symbols and words of the thoughts which the passing events shall awaken. At the call of a noble sentiment, again the woods wave, the pines murmur, the river rolls and shines, and the cattle low upon the mountains, as he saw and heard them in his infancy. And with these forms, the spells of persuasion, the keys of power are put into his hands.

From NATURE

James Middleton

Agriculture is the venerable mother of all the arts an civilized society. . .

Agriculture is the venerable mother of all the arts and the foundation, among them, of civilized society. For, this first banded men together, to make conventions for the security of property, and this also will last the longest, because when the world is too full for pasture or hunting, men must still derive their whole subsistence from the ground . . . A reputation for solid qualities of mind has been conceded to the husbandman by universal consent. He is deemed trustworthy, reflecting, substantial, and pious; headstrong perchance in his bigotries, but for like reasons firm [and] constant in his affections and principles.

Journal, 1822

54

Emerson thought that everything, a cornfield for example, would unlock a new faculty of the soul when rightly seen.

the foundation of

A life in harmony with Nature, the love of truth and of virtue, will purge the eyes to understand her text. By degrees we may come to know the primitive sense of the permanent objects of nature, so that the world shall be to us an open book, and every form significant of its hidden life and final cause.

A new interest surprises us, whilst, under the view now suggested, we contemplate the fearful extent and multitude of objects; since "every object rightly seen, unlocks a new faculty of the soul." That which was unconscious truth, becomes, when interpreted and defined in an object, a part of the domain of knowledge — a new weapon in the magazine of power.

From NATURE

John M. Zielinski

"...Every man has an exceptional
respect for tillage, and a feeling that
this is the original calling of his race.

The glory of the farmer is that, in the division of labors, it is his part to create. All trade rests at last on his primitive activity. He stands close to Nature; he obtains from the earth the bread and the meat. The food which was not, he causes to be. The first farmer was the first man, and all historic nobility rests on possession and use of land. Men do not like hard work, but every man has an exceptional respect for tillage, and a feeling that this is the original calling of his race, that he himself is only excused from it by some circumstance which made him delegate it for a time to other hands. If he have not some skill which recommends him to the farmer, some product for which the farmer will give him corn, he must himself return into his due place among the planters. And the profession has in all eyes its ancient charm, as standing nearest to God, the first cause.

The farmer stands close to Nature; he obtains from the earth the bread and the meat. . .

Then the beauty of Nature, the tranquility and innocence of the countryman, his independence and his pleasing arts — the care of bees, of poultry, of sheep, of cows, the dairy, the care of hay, of fruits, of orchards and forests, and the reaction of these on the workman, in giving him a strength and plain dignity like the face and manners of Nature — all men acknowledge.

From SOCIETY AND SOLITUDE

The hurts of the husbandmen are many. As soon as the heat bursts his vine-seed and the cotyledons open, the striped yellow bugs and the stupid squash-bug, smelling like a decomposing pear, sting the little plants to death and destroy the hope of melons. And as soon as the grass is well cut and spread on the ground, the thunderclouds, which are the bugs of the haymakers, come growling down the heaven and make tea of his hay.

Journal, April 1843

"The good of doing with one's own hands is the honoring of the symbol. My own cooking, my own cobbling, fencebuilding . . . — is poetic."

Howard Sochurek

When a man has got to a certain point in his career of truth he becomes conscious forevermore that he must take himself for better or worse as his portion, that what he can get out of his plot of ground by the sweat of his brow is his meat, and though the wide universe is full of good, not a particle can he add to himself but through his toil bestowed on this spot. It looks to him indeed a little spot, a poor barren possession, filled with thorns and a lurking place for adders and apes and wolves. But cultivation will work wonders. It will enlarge to his eye as it is explored. That little nook will swell to a world of light and power and love.

Journal, 1830

The good of doing with one's own hands is the honoring of the symbol. My own cooking, my own cobbling, fence-building, digging of a well, building of a house, twisting of a rope, forging of a hoe and shovel — is poetic.

Journal, 1845

I dissected the buds of the birch and the oak . . .

We are far from having exhausted the significance of the few symbols we use. We can come to use them yet with a terrible simplicity. It does not need that a poem should be long. Every word was once a poem. Every new relation is a new word. Also we use defects and deformities to a sacred purpose, so expressing our sense that the evils of the world are such only to the evil eye. In the old mythology, mythologists observe, defects are ascribed to divine natures, as lameness to Vulcan, blindness to Cupid, and the like — to signify exuberances.

For as it is dislocation and detachment from the life of God that makes things ugly, the poet, who re-attaches things to nature and the Whole — re-attaching even artificial things and violation of nature, to nature, by a deeper insight — disposes very easily of the most disagreeable facts.

From "The Poet," ESSAYS: SECOND SERIES

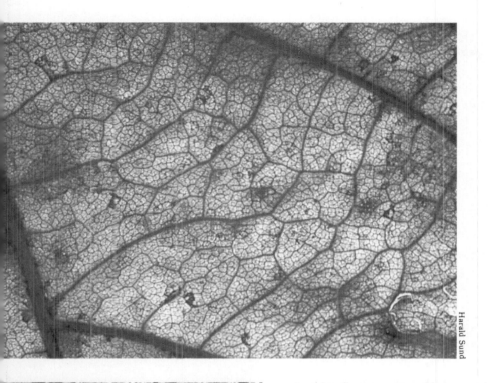

Harald Sund

S.J. Krasemann

A robber fly on a yarrow blossom, a leaf and a deformed
stump — it is the poet, Emerson thought, "who re-attaches things to
nature and the Whole — re-attaching even artificial things and
violation of nature, to nature, by a deeper insight —
disposes very easily of the most disagreeable facts."

The ruin or the blank that we see when we look at nature
is in our own eye. The axis of vision is not coincident with
the axis of things, and so they appear not transparent but
opaque. The reason why the world lacks unity, and lies
broken and in heaps, is because man is disunited with
himself. He cannot be a naturalist until he satisfies all the
demands of the spirit. Love is as much its demand as
perception. Indeed, neither can be perfect without the other.
In the uttermost meaning of the words, thought is devout and
devotion is thought. Deep calls unto deep. But in actual life,
the marriage is not celebrated. There are innocent men who
worship God after the tradition of their fathers, but their
sense of duty has not yet extended to the use of all their
faculties. And there are patient naturalists, but they freeze
their subject under the wintry light of the understanding. Is
not prayer also a study of truth — a sally of the soul into the
unfound infinite? No man ever prayed heartily without
learning something. But when a faithful thinker, resolute to
detach every object from personal relations and see it in the
light of thought, shall, at the same time, kindle science with
the fire of the holiest affections, then will God go forth anew
into the creation. . . .

From NATURE

It is very unhappy, but too late to be helped, the discovery we have made that we exist. That discovery is called the Fall of Man. Ever afterwards we suspect our instruments. . . . Never can love make consciousness and ascription equal in force.

From "Experience," ESSAYS: SECOND SERIES

I hold our actual knowledge very cheap. Hear the rats in the wall, see the lizards on the fence, the fungus under foot, the lichen on the log. What do I know sympathetically, morally, of either of these worlds of life? As old as the Caucasian man — perhaps older — these creatures have kept their counsel beside him, and there is no record of any word or sign that has passed from one to the other. What connection do the books show between the fifty or sixty chemical elements and the historical eras? Nay what does history yet record of the metaphysical annals of man? What light does it shed on those mysteries which we hide under the names Death and Immortality? Yet every history should be written in a wisdom which divined the range of our affinities and looked at facts as symbols. I am ashamed to see what a shallow village tale our so-called history is. How many times we must say Rome, and Paris, and Constantinople!

From "History," ESSAYS: FIRST SERIES

If life were long enough, among my thousands and one works should be a book of nature whereof Howitt's *Seasons* should be not so much the model as the parody. It should contain the natural history of the woods around my shifting camp for every month in the year. It should tie their astronomy, botany, physiology, meteorology, picturesque, and poetry together. No bird, no bug, no bud, should be forgotten on his day and hour. To-day the chickadees, the robins, bluebirds and song-sparrows sang to me. I dissected the buds of the birch and the oak; in every one of the last is a star. The crow sat above as idle as I below. The river flowed brimful, and I philosophised upon this composite, collective beauty which refuses to be analysed. Nothing is beautiful alone. Nothing but is beautiful in the whole. Learn the history of a cranberry. Mark the day when the pine cones and acorns fall.

Journal, 1835

"Nothing is beautiful alone. Nothing but is beautiful in the whole."

David Trumbel

IV
A Prodigality
of Seeds

The charm of life is this variety of genius, these contrasts and flavors by which Heaven has modulated the identity of truth, and there is a perpetual hankering to violate this individuality, to warp his ways. . . to resemble your thinking and behavior. . . . You are trying to make that other man you. One's enough.

T.D. Lowes

I have no hostility to nature, but a child's love to it...

. . . Nature does not like to be observed, and likes that we should be her fools and playmates. We may have the sphere for our cricket-ball, but not a berry for our philosophy. Direct strokes she never gave us power to make; all our blows glance, all our hits are accidents. Our relations to each other are oblique and casual.

From "Experience," ESSAYS: SECOND SERIES

. . . A man should think much of himself because he is a necessary being; a link was wanting between two craving parts of nature and he was hurled into being as the bridge, over that yawning need. . . .

From "The Method of Nature," Lecture, 1841

"Nature is no sentimentalist — does not cosset or pamper us. We must see that the world is rough and surly."

*More servants wait on man
Than he'll take notice of.
— George Herbert*

Nature, in its ministry to man, is not only the material, but is also the process and the result. All the parts incessantly work into each other's hands for the profit of man. The wind sows the seed; the sun evaporates the sea; the wind blows the vapor to the field; the ice, on the other side of the planet, condenses rain on this; the rain feeds the plant; the plant feeds the animal; and thus the endless circulation of the divine charity nourishes man. . . .

I have no hostility to nature, but a child's love to it. I expand and live in the warm day like corn and melons. Let us speak her fair. I do not wish to fling stones at my beautiful mother, nor soil my gentle nest. I only wish to indicate the true position of nature in regard to man, wherein to establish man all right education tends; as the ground which to attain is the object of human life, that is, of man's connection with nature.

From NATURE

David Trumbel

". . . Nature does not like to be observed and likes that we should be her fools and playmates."

. . . Nature is no sentimentalist — does not cosset or pamper us. We must see that the world is rough and surly, and will not mind drowning a man or a woman, but swallows your ship like a grain of dust.

From CONDUCT OF LIFE

. . . Life takes its color and quality not from the days, but the dawns. The lucid intervals are like drowning men's moments, equivalent to the foregoing years. Besides, Nature uses us. We live but little for ourselves, a good deal for our children, and strangers: Each man is one more lump of clay to hold the world together.

Letter to Thomas Carlyle

What is a man but nature's finer success in self-explication?
From "ART," ESSAYS: FIRST SERIES

65

The vegetable life fills the air and earth with a prodigality of seeds...

. . . Men are not made like boxes, a hundred or thousand to order, and all exactly alike, of known dimension, and all their properties known; but no, they come into nature through a nine months' astonishment, and of a character, each one, incalculable, and of extravagant possibilities. Out of darkness and out of the awful Cause they come to be caught up into this vision of a seeing, partaking, acting and suffering life, not foreknown, not fore-estimable, but slowly or speedily they unfold new, unknown, mighty traits: not boxes, but these machines are alive, agitated, fearing, sorrowing.

Journal, November 12, 1838

"Nature never rhymes her children, nor makes two men alike."

Robert Sena

Divine persons are character born, or, to borrow a phrase from Napoleon, they are victory organized. They are usually received with ill-will, because they are new and because they set a bound to the exaggeration that has been made of the personality of the last divine person. Nature never rhymes her children, nor makes two men alike.

From "Character," ESSAYS: SECOND SERIES

The charm of life is this variety of genius, these contrasts and flavors by which Heaven has modulated the identity of truth, and there is a perpetual hankering to violate this individuality, to warp his ways of thinking and behavior to resemble or reflect your thinking and behavior. A low self-love in the parent desires that his child should repeat his character and fortune; an expectation which the child, if justice is done him, will nobly disappoint. By working on the theory that this resemblance exists, we shall do what in us lies to defeat his proper promise and produce the ordinary and mediocre. I suffer whenever I see that common sight of a parent or senior imposing his opinion and way of thinking and being on a young soul to which they are totally unfit. Cannot we let people be themselves, and enjoy life in their own way? You are trying to make that man another *you*. One's enough.

From EDUCATION

*Of the many poison ivy seeds
in these berries, hundreds may come up
that tens may live to maturity.*

The vegetable life does not content itself with casting from the flower or the tree a single seed, but it fills the air and earth with a prodigality of seeds, that, if thousands perish, thousands may plant themselves, that hundreds may come up that tens may live to maturity, that, at least, one may replace the parent.

From "Nature," ESSAYS: SECOND SERIES

My life is a May game, I will live as I like. I defy your strait-laced, weary, social ways and modes. Blue is the sky, green the fields and groves, fresh the springs, glad the rivers, and hospitable the splendor of sun and star. I will play my game out. And if any shall say me nay, shall come out with swords and staves against me to prick me to death for their foolish laws — come and welcome. I will not look grave for such a fool's matter. I cannot lose my cheer for such trumpery. Life is a May game still.

Journal, June 6, 1839

Unpublished nature will have its whole secret told...

Whenever the pulpit is usurped by a formalist, then is the worshipper defrauded and disconsolate. We shrink as soon as the prayers begin, which do not uplift, but smite and offend us. We are fain to wrap our cloaks about us, and secure, as best we can, a solitude that hears not. I once heard a preacher who sorely tempted me to say I would go to church no more. Men go, thought I, where they are wont to go, else had no soul entered the temple in the afternoon. A snow-storm was falling around us. The snow-storm was real, the preacher merely spectral, and the eye felt the sad contrast in looking at him, and then out of the window behind him into the beautiful meteor of the snow.

From An address delivered before the Senior Class at
Divinity College, Cambridge, July 1838

The event of death is always astounding; our philosophy never reaches, never possesses it; we are always at the beginning of our catechism; always the definition is yet to be made. What is death?

Journal, October 28, 1837

Nothing is left us now but death. We look to that with a grim satisfaction, saying, There at least is reality that will not dodge us.

From "Experience," ESSAYS: SECOND SERIES

Beautiful as is the symmetry of any form, if the form can move we seek a more excellent symmetry. The interruption of equilibrium stimulates the eye to desire the restoration of symmetry, and to watch the steps through which it is attained. This is the charm of running water, sea waves, the flight of birds and the locomotion of animals. This is the theory of dancing, to recover continually in changes the lost equilibrium, not by abrupt and angular but by gradual and curving movements. . . . This fact suggests the reason of all mistakes and offence in our own modes. It is necessary in music, when you strike a discord, to let down the ear by an intermediate note or two to the accord again: and many a

For Emerson, the charm of running water was its movement, for the interruption of equilibrium stimulated his eye to seek the restoration of symmetry.

good experiment, born of good sense and destined to succeed, fails only because it is offensively sudden. . . . To this streaming or flowing belongs the beauty that all circular movement has; as the circulation of waters, the circulation of the blood, the periodical motion of planets, the annual wave of vegetation, the action and reaction of nature; and if we follow it out, this demand in our thought for an ever onward action is the argument for the immortality.

From CONDUCT OF LIFE

Man, made of the dust of the world, does not forget his origin; and all that is yet inanimate will one day speak and reason. Unpublished nature will have its whole secret told.

Thus we sit by the fire and take hold on the poles of the earth.

From REPRESENTATIVE MEN

A Vision of the Whole

V

Although the works of nature are innumerable and all different, the result or the expression of them all is similar and single. Nature is a sea of forms radically alike and even unique. A leaf, a sunbeam, a landscape, the ocean, make an analogous impression on the mind. What is common to them all . . . is beauty.

Nature never wears a mean appearance. . .

A nobler want of man is served by nature, namely, the love of Beauty.

From NATURE

Things are pretty, graceful, rich, elegant, handsome, but, until they speak to the imagination, not yet beautiful. This is the reason why beauty is still escaping out of all analysis. It is not yet possessed, it cannot be handled. Proclus says, "It swims on the light of forms." It is properly not in the form, but in the mind. It instantly deserts possession, and flies to an object in the horizon. If I could put my hand on the North Star, would it be as beautiful? The sea is lovely, but when we bathe in it the beauty forsakes all the near water. For the imagination and senses cannot be gratified at the same time. Wordsworth rightly speaks of "a light that never was on sea or land," meaning that it was supplied by the observer; and the Welsh bard warns his countrywomen, that
     — "half of their charms with Cadwallon shall die."
The new virtue which constitutes a thing beautiful is a certain cosmical quality, or a power to suggest relation to the whole world, and so lift the object out of a pitiful individuality.

From CONDUCT OF LIFE

The stars awaken a certain reverence, because though always present, they are inaccessible; but all natural objects make a kindred impression, when the mind is open to their influence. Nature never wears a mean appearance. Neither does the wisest man extort her secret, and lose his curiosity by finding out all her perfection. Nature never became a toy to a wise spirit. The flowers, the animals, the mountains, reflected the wisdom of his best hour, as much as they had delighted the simplicity of his childhood.

When we speak of nature in this manner, we have a distinct but most poetical sense in the mind. We mean the integrity of impression made by manifold natural objects. It is this which distinguishes the stick of timber of the woodcutter from the tree of the poet.

From NATURE

"The stars awaken a certain reverence, because . . . they are inaccessible."

Nature always wears the colors of the spirit...

Harald Sund

"The sky is less grand as it shuts down over less worth in the population."

74

Have mountains, and waves, and skies, no significance but what we consciously give them when we employ them as emblems of our thoughts? The world is emblematic. Parts of speech are metaphors, because the whole of nature is a metaphor of the human mind. The laws of moral nature answer to those of matter as face to face in a glass. . . .

This relation between the mind and matter is not fancied by some poet, but stands in the will of God, and so is free to be known by all men. It appears to men, or it does not appear. When in fortunate hours we ponder this miracle, the wise man doubts if at all other times he is not blind and deaf; . . . for the universe becomes transparent, and the light of higher laws than its own shines through it.

From NATURE

. . . Nature always wears the colors of the spirit. To a man laboring under calamity, the heat of his own fire hath sadness in it. Then there is a kind of contempt of the landscape felt by him who has just lost by death a dear friend. The sky is less grand as it shuts down over less worth in the population.

From NATURE

The papery blossoms of the California poppy are such a brilliant yellow that they nearly dazzle the viewer.

T.D. Lowes

Robert L. Olsen

Each particle is a microcosm, and faithfully renders the likeness of the world. . .

Sensible objects conform to the premonitions of Reason and reflect the conscience. All things are moral; and in their boundless changes have an unceasing reference to spiritual nature. Therefore is nature glorious with form, color, and motion. . . .

Herein is especially apprehended the unity of Nature — the unity in variety — which meets us everywhere. All the endless variety of things make an identical impression. Xenophanes complained in his old age, that, look where he would, all things hastened back to Unity. He was weary of seeing the same entity in the tedious variety of forms. The fable of Proteus has a cordial truth. A leaf, a drop, a crystal, a moment of time, is related to the whole, and partakes of the perfection of the whole. Each particle is a microcosm, and faithfully renders the likeness of the world.

From NATURE

. . . There will be the same gulf between every me and thee as between the original and the picture. The universe is the bride of the soul. All private sympathy is partial. Two human beings are like globes, which can touch only in a point, and whilst they remain in contact all other points of each of the spheres are inert; their turn must also come, and the longer a particular union lasts the more energy of appetency the parts not in union acquire.

From "Experience," ESSAYS: SECOND SERIES

The first care of a man settling in the country should be to open the face of the earth to himself by a little knowledge of nature, or a great deal, if he can; of birds, plants, rocks, astronomy; in short, the art of taking a walk. This will draw the sting out of frost, dreariness out of November and March, and the drowsiness out of August.

From LETTERS AND SOCIAL AIMS

"A leaf . . . is related to the whole, and partakes of the perfection of the whole."

There is no object so foul
that intense light will
not make beautiful . . .

There is no object so foul that intense light will not make beautiful. . . . But besides this general grace diffused over nature, almost all the individual forms are agreeable to the eye, as is proved by our endless imitations of some of them, as the acorn, the grape, the pine cone, the wheat-ear, the egg, the wings and forms of most birds, the lion's claw, the serpent, the butterfly, sea-shells, flames, clouds, buds, leaves, and the forms of many trees, as the palm.

From NATURE

The Gothic church plainly originated in a rude adaptation of the forest trees, with all their boughs, to a festal or solemn arcade; as the bands about the cleft pillars still indicate the green withes that tied them. No one can walk in a road cut through pine woods, without being struck with the architectural appearance of the grove, especially in winter, when the barrenness of all other trees shows the low arch of the Saxons. In the woods in a winter afternoon one will see as readily the origin of the stained glass window with which the Gothic cathedrals are adorned, in the colors of the western sky seen through the bare and crossing branches of the forest. Nor can any lover of nature enter the old piles of Oxford and the English cathedrals, without feeling that the forest overpowered the mind of the builder, and that his chisel, his saw and plane still reproduced its ferns, its spikes of flowers, its locust, elm, oak, pine, fir and spruce.

The Gothic cathedral is a blossoming in stone subdued by the insatiable demand of harmony in man. The mountain of granite blooms into an eternal flower, with the lightness and delicate finish, as well as the aerial proportions and perspective, of vegetable beauty.

From "History," ESSAYS: FIRST SERIES

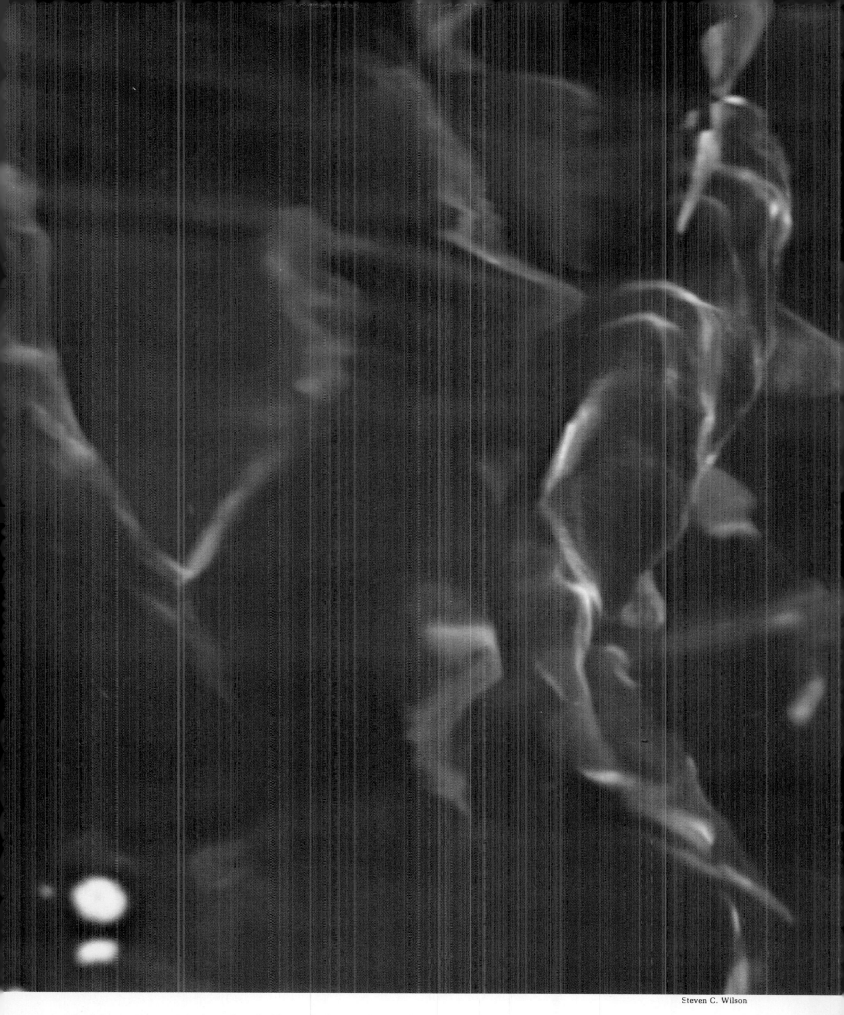

At the spawning period, the ordinarily blue and silver sockeye salmon turns red.

Nature is a sea of forms radically alike and even unique...

. . . A work of art is an abstract or epitome of the world. It is the result or expression of nature, in miniature. For although the works of nature are innumerable and all different, the result or the expression of them all is similar and single. Nature is a sea of forms radically alike and even unique. A leaf, a sunbeam, a landscape, the ocean, make an analogous impression on the mind. What is common to them all — that perfectness and harmony, is beauty. The standard of beauty is the entire circuit of natural forms — the totality of nature; which the Italians expressed by defining beauty *il pie nell' uno.* Nothing is quite beautiful alone; nothing but is beautiful in the whole. A single object is only so far beautiful as it suggests this universal grace. The poet, the painter, the sculptor, the musician, the architect, seek each to concentrate this radiance of the world on one point and each in his several works to satisfy the love of beauty which stimulates him to produce. Thus is Art a nature passed through the alembic of man. Thus in art does Nature work through the will of a man filled with the beauty of her first works.

The world thus exists to the soul to satisfy the desire of beauty. This element I call an ultimate end. No reason can be asked or given why the soul seeks beauty. Beauty, in its largest and profoundest sense, is one expression for the universe. God is the all-fair. Truth, and goodness, and beauty, are but different faces of the same All. But beauty in nature is not ultimate. It is the herald of inward and eternal beauty, and is not alone a solid and satisfactory good. It must stand as a part, and not as yet the last or highest expression of the final cause of Nature.

From NATURE

. . . Every word which is used to express a moral or intellectual fact, if traced to its root, is found to be borrowed from some material appearance. *Right* means *straight; wrong* means *twisted; spirit* primarily means *wind.*
. . . Who looks upon a river in a meditative hour and is not reminded of the flux of all things? Throw a stone into the stream, and the circles that propagate themselves are the beautiful type of all influence. Man is conscious of a universal soul within or behind his individual life, wherein, as in a firmament, the natures of Justice, Truth, Love,

"Throw a stone into the stream, and the circles that propagate themselves are the beautiful types of all influence."

Helen Nestor

80

". . . Who looks upon a river in a meditative hour and is not reminded of the flux of all things?"

Freedom, arise and shine. This universal soul he calls Reason: it is not mine, or thine, or his, but we are its; we are its property and men. And the blue sky in which the private earth is buried, the sky with its eternal calm, and full of everlasting orbs, is the type of Reason. That which intellectually considered we call Reason, considered in relation to nature, we call Spirit. Spirit is the Creator. Spirit hath life in itself. And man in all ages and countries embodies it in his language as the *Father.* Father. FATHER.

From NATURE

81

VI
"All the Trees are Wind-harps"

The mind loves its old home: as water to our thirst, so is the rock, the ground, to our eyes, and hands, and feet. It is firm water: it is cold flame: what health, what affinity! . . . Cities give not the human senses room enough. . . .

Philip Steinmetz

Transcendancy: In a cotillon some persons dance and others await their turn when the music and the figure come to them. In the dance of God there is not one of the chorus but can and will begin to spin, monumental as he now looks, whenever the music and figure reach his place and duty. O celestial Bacchus! drive them mad — this multitude of vagabonds, hungry for eloquence, hungry for poetry, starving for symbols, perishing for want of electricity to vitalize this too much pasture, and in the long delay indemnifying themselves with the false wine of alcohol, of politics or of money. . . .

The poet is representative _ whole man, diamond-merchant, symbolizer, emancipator . . .

. . . The poet is representative — whole man, diamond-merchant, symbolizer, emancipator; in him the world projects a scribe's hand and writes the adequate genesis. The nature of things is flowing, a metamorphosis. The free spirit sympathizes not only with the actual form, but with the power or possible forms; but for obvious municipal or parietal uses God has given us a bias or a rest on today's forms. Hence the shudder of joy with which in each clear moment we recognize the metamorphosis, because it is always a conquest, a surprise from the heart of things.

From LETTERS AND SOCIAL AIMS

. . . Look, look, old mole! there, straight up before you, is the magnificent Sun. If only for the instant, you see it. Well, in this way it educates the youth of the universe; in this way warms, suns, refines every particle; then it drops the little channel or canal, through which the Life rolled beatific, like a fossil to the ground, thus touched and educated, by a moment of sunshine, to be the fairer material for future channels and canals, through which the old Glory shall dart again, in new directions, until the Universe shall have been shot through and through, *tilled* with light. . . .

Journal, July 1852

The poet's own body is a fleeing apparition — his personality as fugitive as the trope he employs. In certain hours we can almost pass our hand through our own body.

From LETTERS AND SOCIAL AIMS

Went yesterday to Cambridge and spent most of the day at Mount Auburn; got my luncheon at Fresh Pond, and went back again to the woods. After much wandering and seeing many things, four snakes gliding up and down a hollow for no purpose that I could see — not to eat, not for love, but only gliding; then a whole bed of *Hepatica triloba*, cousin of the Anemone, all blue and beautiful, but constrained by niggard nature to wear their last year's faded jacket of leaves; then a black-capped titmouse, who came upon a tree, and when I would know his name, sang *chick-a-dee-dee;* then a far-off tree full of clamorous birds, I know not what, but you might hear them half a mile. I forsook the tombs,

Stone Photography

*The man . . . who rambles in the woods,
seems to be the first man that ever . . .
entered a grove. Go into the forest,
you shall find all new and undescribed.*

and found a sunny hollow where the east wind would not blow, and lay down against the side of a tree to most happy beholdings. At least I opened my eyes and let what would pass through them into the soul. I saw no more my relation, how near and petty, to Cambridge or Boston; I heeded no more what minute or hour our Massachusetts clocks might indicate — I saw only the noble earth on which I was born, with the great Star which warms and enlightens it. I saw the clouds that hang their significant drapery over us. It was Day — that was all Heaven said. . . .

See the perpetual generation of good sense: nothing wholly false, fantastic, can take possession of men who, to live and move, must plough the ground, sail the sea, have orchards, hear the robin sing, and see the swallow fly.

Journal, April 11, 1834

86

Go into the forest, you shall find all new and undescribed...

... Go into the forest, you shall find all new and undescribed. The honking of the wild geese flying by night; the thin note of the companionable titmouse in the winter day; the fall of swarms of flies, in autumn, from combats high in the air, pattering down on the leaves like rain; the angry hiss of the wood-birds; the pine throwing out its pollen for the benefit of the next century; the turpentine exuding from the tree — and indeed any vegetation, any animation, any and all, are alike unattempted. The man who stands on the seashore, or who rambles in the woods, seems to be the first man that ever stood on the shore, or entered a grove, his sensations and his world are so novel and strange. Whilst I read the poets, I think that nothing new can be said about morning and evening. But when I see the daybreak I am not reminded of these Homeric, or Shakespearean, or Miltonic, or Chaucerian pictures. No; but I feel perhaps the pain of an alien world; a world not yet subdued by the thought; or I am cheered by the moist, warm, glittering, budding, melodious hour, that takes down the narrow walls of my soul, and extends its life and pulsation to the very horizon. That is morning, to cease for a bright hour to be a prisoner of this sickly body, and to become as large as nature.

From "Literary Ethics," Lecture, 1838

I dreamed that I floated at will in the great Ether, and I saw this world floating also not far off, but diminished to the size of an apple. Then an angel took it in his hand and brought it to me and said, "This must thou eat." And I ate the world.

Journal, October 24, 1840

I went into the woods. I found myself not wholly present there. If I looked at a pine-tree or an aster, *that* did not seem to be nature. Nature was still elsewhere: this, or this was but outskirt and far-off reflection and echo of the triumph that had passed by and was now at its glancing splendor and heyday — perchance in the neighboring fields, or, if I stood in the field, then in the adjacent woods. Always the present object gave me this sense of the stillness that follows a pageant that has just gone by.

Journal, September, 1840

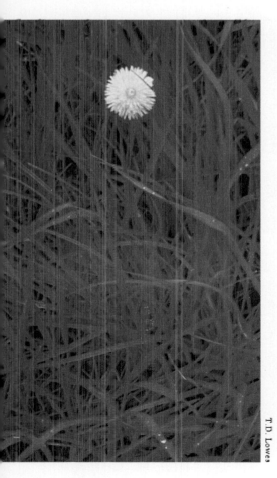

"I went into the woods. Nature was still elsewhere: this, or this was but outskirt and far-off reflection and echo of the triumph that had passed by."

An enchanting night of south wind and clouds; mercury at 73 degrees; all the trees are wind-harps; blessed be light and darkness; ebb and flow, cold and heat; these restless pulsations of nature which by and by will throb no more.

Journal, August 2, 1837

Thoughts let us into realities. Neither miracle nor magic nor any religious tradition, not the immortality of the private soul is incredible, after we have experienced an insight, a thought. I think it comes to some men but once in their life, sometimes a religious impulse, sometimes an intellectual insight. But what we want is consecutiveness. 'Tis with us a flash of light, then a long darkness, then a flash again. The separation of our days by sleep almost destroys identity. Could we but turn these fugitive sparkles into an astronomy of Copernican worlds! . . . We cannot make the inspiration consecutive. . . . Sometimes there is no sea-fire, and again the sea is aglow to the horizon. Sometimes the Aeolian harp is dumb all day in the window, and again it is garrulous and tells all the secrets of the world. In June the morning is noisy with birds; in August they are already getting old and silent.

From LETTERS AND SOCIAL AIMS

". . . Dry leaves hiss; grass bends and rustles, and I have died out of the human world and come to feel a strange, cold, aqueous, . . . existence.

Philip Steinmetz

*"But the sublime light of night
is unsatisfying, provoking; it
astonishes but explains not."*

Last night the moon rose behind four distinct pine-tree tops in the distant woods and the night at ten was so bright that I walked abroad. But the sublime light of night is unsatisfying, provoking; it astonishes but explains not. Its charm floats, dances, disappears, comes and goes, but palls in five minutes after you have left the house. Come out of your warm, angular house, resounding with few voices, into the chill, grand, instantaneous night, with such a Presence as a full moon in the clouds, and you are struck with poetic wonder. In the instant you leave far behind all human relations, wife, mother and child, and live only with the savages — water, air, light, carbon, lime, and granite. . . . I become a moist, cold element. "Nature grows over me." Frogs pipe; waters far off tinkle; dry leaves hiss; grass bends and rustles, and I have died out of the human world and come to feel a strange, cold, aqueous, terraqueous, aerial, ethereal sympathy and existence. I sow the sun and moon for seeds.

Journal, May 11, 1838

We learn nothing rightly until we learn the symbolical character of life. Day creeps after day, each full of facts, dull, strange, despised things, that we cannot enough despise — call heavy, prosaic and desert. The time we seek to kill: the attention it is elegant to divert from things around us. And presently the aroused intellect finds cold and gems in one of these scorned facts — then finds that the day of facts is a rock of diamonds; that a fact is an Epiphany of God.

From EDUCATION

As water to our thirst, so is the ground to our eyes, and hands, and feet...

There are days which occur in this climate, at almost any season of the year, wherein the world reaches its perfection, when the air, the heavenly bodies, and the earth make a harmony, as if nature would indulge her offspring; . . . Here we find nature to be the circumstance which dwarfs every other circumstance, and judges like a god all men that come to her. . . . The tempered light of the woods is like a perpetual morning, and is stimulating and heroic. The anciently reported spells of these places creep on us. The stems of pines, hemlocks, and oaks, almost gleam like iron on the excited eye. The incommunicable trees begin to persuade us to live with them, and quit our life of solemn trifles. Here no history, or church, or state, is interpolated on the divine sky and the immortal year. . . .

We never can part with it; the mind loves its old home: as water to our thirst, so is the rock, the ground, to our eyes, and hands, and feet. It is firm water: it is cold flame: what health, what affinity! . . . Cities give not the human senses room enough. . . .

From "Nature," ESSAYS: SECOND SERIES

The world globes itself in a drop of dew. The microscope cannot find the animalcule which is less perfect for being little. Eyes, ears, taste, smell, motion, resistance, appetite, and organs of reproduction that take hold on eternity — all find room to consist in the small creature. So do we put our life into every act. The true doctrine of omnipresence is that God reappears with all his parts in every moss and cobweb.

From "Compensation," ESSAYS: FIRST SERIES

It is a peculiarity . . . of humour in me, my strong propensity for strolling. I deliberately shut up my books in a cloudy July noon, put on my old clothes and old hat and slink away to the whortleberry bushes and slip with the greatest satisfaction into a little cowpath where I am sure I can defy observation. This point gained, I solace myself for hours with picking blue berries and other trash of the woods far from fame behind the birch trees. I seldom enjoy hours as I do these. I remember them in winter; I expect them in spring.

Journal, 1828

The world globes itself in a drop of dew.

In this refulgent summer, it has been a luxury to draw the breath of life. The grass grows, the buds burst, the meadow is spotted with fire and gold in the tint of flowers. The air is full of birds, and sweet with the breath of the pine, the balm-of-Gilead, and the new hay. Night brings no gloom to the heart with its welcome shade.

From An address delivered before
the Senior Class at Divinity School,
Cambridge, July 1838

. . . I see the spectacle of morning from the hill-top over against my house, from day-break to sun-rise, with emotions which an angel might share. The long slender bars of cloud float like fishes in the sea of crimson light. From the earth, as a shore, I look out into that silent sea. I seem to partake its rapid transformations: the active enchantment reaches my dust, and I dilate and conspire with the morning wind. . . .

Not less excellent, except for our less susceptibility in the afternoon, was the charm, last evening, of a January sunset. The western clouds divided and subdivided themselves into pink flakes modulated with tints of unspeakable softness; and the air had so much life and sweetness, that it was a pain to come within doors. What was it that nature would say?

G.R. Johnson

*"I see the spectacle of morning . . .
from day-break to sun-rise with
emotions which an angel might share."*

George T. Manna

Was there no meaning in the live repose of the valley behind the mill, and which Homer or Shakespeare could not re-form for me in words? The leafless trees become spires of flame in the sunset, with the blue east for their back-ground, and the stars of the dead calices of flowers, and every withered stem and stubble rimed with frost, contribute something to the mute music.

The inhabitants of cities suppose that the country landscape is pleasant only half the year. I please myself with the graces of the winter scenery, and believe that we are as much touched by it as by the genial influences of summer. To the attentive eye, each moment of the year has its own beauty, and in the same field, it beholds every hour, a picture which was never seen before, and which shall never be seen again.

From NATURE

93

Beauty breaks in everywhere...

. . . In every landscape, the point of astonishment is the meeting of the sky and the earth, and that is seen from the first hillock as well as from the top of the Alleghenies. The stars at night stoop down over the brownest, homeliest common, with all the spiritual magnificence which they shed on the Campagna, or on the marble deserts of Egypt. The uprolled clouds and the colors of morning and evening, will transfigure maples and alders. The difference between landscape and landscape is small, but there is great difference in the beholders. There is nothing so wonderful in any particular landscape, as the necessity of being beautiful under which every landscape lies. Nature cannot be surprised in undress. Beauty breaks in everywhere.

From "Nature," ESSAYS: SECOND SERIES

In every landscape, the point of astonishment is the meeting of the sky and the earth.

. . . All opaque things are transparent, and the light of heaven struggles through.

Journal, September 11, 1860

Harald Sund

George Johnson

*All opaque things are transparent
and the light of heaven struggles through.*

Spring has returned and has begun to unfold her beautiful array, to throw herself on wild flower couches, to walk abroad on the hills and summon her songsters to do her sweet homage. . . . The poet of course is wandering while nature's thousand melodies are warbling to him. This soft bewitching luxury of vernal gales and accompanying beauty overwhelms. — It produces a lassitude which is full of mental enjoyment and which we would not exchange for more vigorous pleasure. Although so long as the spell endures little or nothing is accomplished, nevertheless, I believe it operates to divest the mind of old and worn-out contemplations and bestows new freshness upon life and leaves behind it imaginations of enchantment. . . .

Journal, 1820

Rohn Engh

In the mists of the morn over many a ridge of pine-covered hills we sought Meredith bridge. The only companions we found on the road were the vervain and aster and Mr. Bryant's golden rod. The mullen though tall looked too much clad for the summer. . . . And the blue Canada thistle was proud of each comer. For the butterflies came to his soft purple nest for reasons not known to those who know best.

Journal, 1829

In the woods is perpetual youth . . .

. . . Nature is a setting that fits equally well a comic or a mourning piece. In good health, the air is a cordial of incredible virtue. Crossing a bare common, in snow puddles, at twilight, under a clouded sky, without having in my thoughts any occurrence of special good fortune, I have enjoyed a perfect exhilaration. I am glad to the brink of fear. In the woods, too, a man casts off his years, as the snake his slough, and at what period soever of life is always a child. In the woods is perpetual youth. . . . In the woods we return to reason and faith. There I feel that nothing can befall me in life — no disgrace, no calamity (leaving me my eyes), which nature cannot repair. Standing on the bare ground — my head bathed by the blithe air, and uplifted into infinite space — all mean egotism vanishes. I become a transparent eyeball; I am nothing; I see all; the currents of the Universal Being circulate through me; I am part or particle of God. The name of the nearest friend sounds then foreign and accidental: to be brothers, to be acquaintances, — master or servant, is then a trifle and a disturbance. . . . In the wilderness, I find something more dear and connate than in streets or villages. In the tranquil landscape, and especially in the distant line of the horizon, man beholds somewhat as beautiful as his own nature.

From NATURE

The doctrine of this Supreme Presence is a cry of joy and exultation. Who shall dare think he has come late into nature, or has missed anything excellent in the past, who seeth the admirable stars of possibility, and the yet un-touched continent of hope glittering with all its mountains in the vast West? I praise with wonder this great reality which seems to drown all things in the deluge of its light.

From "The Method of Nature." Lecture, 1841

I said when I awoke, After some more sleepings and wakings I shall lie on this mattress sick; then, dead; and through my gay entry they will carry these bones. Where shall I be then? I lifted my head and beheld the spotless orange light of the morning beaming up from the dark hills into the wide Universe.

Journal, 1837

Photo by W.J. Winkie